Science Alive

Sound

Terry Jennings

SAUNDERS
BOOK COMPANY

Published by Saunders Book Company
27 Stewart Road
Collingwood, ON Canada L9Y 4M7

Created by Q2A Media
Series Editor: Honor Head
Book Editor: Katie Dicker
Senior Art Designer: Ashita Murgai, Nishant Mudgal
Designer: Harleen Mehta
Picture Researchers: Poloumi Ghosh
Line Artists: Indernil Ganguly, Rishi Bhardhwaj
Illustrators: Kusum Kala, Manish Prasad, Sanyogita Lal

Library of Congress Cataloging-in-Publication Data

Jennings, Terry J.
     Sound / Terry Jennings.
     p. cm.—(Smart Apple Media. Science alive)
Summary: "Explains essential facts about sound, including human voices, how musical instruments work, echoes, and ultrasound. Includes experiments"—Provided by publisher.
     Includes index.
     ISBN 978-1-897563-59-5
     1. Sounds—Juvenile literature. 2. Sound—Juvenile literature. 3. Sound-waves—Juvenile literature. 4. Music—Acoustics and physics—Juvenile literature. 5. Hearing—Juvenile literature. 6. Ultrasonics—Juvenile literature. I. Title.
QC225.5.J458 2009
534—dc22
                                                                                                2007043679

All words in **bold** can be found in "Words to Remember" on pages 30–31.

Web site information is correct at time of going to press. However, the publishers cannot accept liability for any information or links found on third-party web sites.

Picture credits
t=top b=bottom c=center l=left r=right m=middle
Cover Images: : Main Image: Ron Levine/ The Image Bank / Getty images   Small Image: Marcel Mooij / Shutterstock: Andrew Johnson/ Istockphoto: 4b, A. Inden /zefa/ Corbis: 5l, Nasa: 6m, paulaphoto/ Shutterstock: 10b, Tom Stewart/Corbis: 14b, ACE STOCK LIMITED / Alamy: 15b, David Sailors/Corbis: 19, misha shiyanov/ Istockphoto: 20l, Xtreme safari Inc./ Shutterstock: 21m, Richard T. Nowitz/ Corbis: 24b, Mira / Alamy: 27b, Picture Press/ Photolibrary: 29t.

Printed in the United States of America in North Mankato, Minnesota
112009
DAD0023

9 8 7 6 5 4 3 2

Contents

What Is Sound? 4

Moving Sounds 6

Try This… Seeing Sound 8

Voices 10

Try This… Different Sounds 12

Making Music 14

Try This… Rubber Band Guitar 16

Hearing 18

Animals' Hearing 20

Try This… String Telephone 22

Echoes 24

Ultrasound 26

Seeing with Sound 28

Words to Remember 30

Index 32

Web Finder 32

What Is Sound?

Our world is full of different sounds.
Sounds help us **communicate** and
can also warn us of danger.

Making Sounds

Sounds are made when something **vibrates,**
or shakes. The vibrations make the air shake
as well. When the shaking air enters our
ears, we hear the sound as a noise.

◀ *We call the
vibrations of air
"sound waves."
They move in a
similar way to
ripples of water
spreading across
a pond.*

Different Sounds

Sounds can be loud or soft. Sounds can also be high and low. When a mouse squeaks, it makes a very high sound, but when a cow moos, it makes a very low sound. High and low sounds are said to have a different "**pitch.**"

◀ *Musical instruments can make loud and soft sounds and high and low notes. If you play a piano, you have lots of notes to choose from.*

Moving Sounds

Most of the time, the sounds that we hear are traveling through air. Air is a gas, but sounds can travel through liquids and solids, too.

▲ *There is no sound in space. This is because there is nothing for sound waves to travel through. Astronauts can communicate in space because their helmets turn sound waves into radio waves.*

The Speed of Sound

Sound travels through the air at about 1,115 ft (340 m) per second. It moves even faster through solids and liquids. If you put your ear against the top of a solid table and tap the table with a coin, you will hear the sound very clearly. Underwater, a whale's song can travel hundreds of miles to reach other whales.

▼ *The sound of this balloon bursting reaches the boy's ears almost immediately.*

Try This...

Seeing Sound

Look at how vibrations travel through air and other materials.

You Will Need
• a bowl covered with plastic wrap • a pinch of salt or fine dry sand • a loudspeaker connected to a music system

1 Put the bowl close to the front of the loudspeaker.

2 Sprinkle some salt or dry sand on top of the plastic wrap.

3 Play some music through the loudspeaker. Music with very low notes works best. What happens to the salt or sand?

What happened?

Sound waves from the loudspeaker travel through the air. They cause the air to vibrate, which in turn, causes the plastic wrap to vibrate. The plastic wrap will make a noise, but you probably cannot hear it because of the music. However, you can see the vibrations making the salt or sand move around.

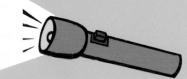

Voices

Every day we make sounds to communicate with other people. We can make loud and soft sounds and high and low sounds.

All Kinds of Sounds

Most of the sounds that we make are with our voice. We can talk, shout, sing, and whisper. Just by taking a breath of air, we can make any sound we want.

▼ *A singer uses her voice to make lots of different sounds. Her voice is like a musical instrument.*

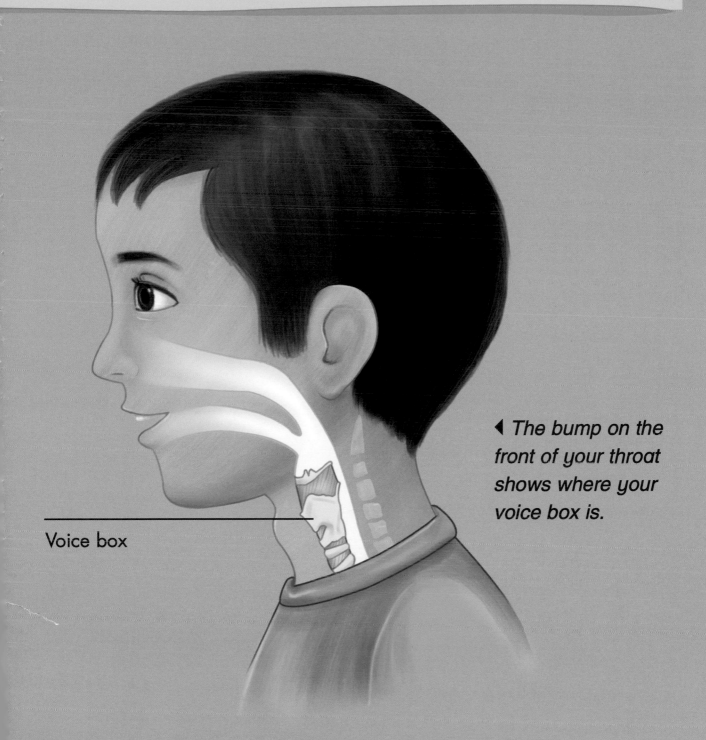

Voice box

◀ The bump on the front of your throat shows where your voice box is.

The Voice Box

When we breathe in and out, air goes through our **voice box.** This can make tiny cords vibrate inside the voice box to produce a humming sound. By moving your mouth, lips, and tongue, you can turn the humming sound into words.

Try This...

Different Sounds

Look at which sounds use the voice box.

You Will Need

No special materials or equipment are needed for this experiment.

1 Put your hand on the front of your throat.

2 Make a zzzzzzzz sound, like the beginning of "zoo" or "zebra."

12

ssss

③ Now make a sssssss sound, like the beginning of "sea" or "snap." What do you notice about the vibrations? Try some other sounds, like "b," "p," "t," and "v."

What happened?

When you make a zzzzzzz sound, you feel the vibrations made by your voice box. But when you make a sssssss sound, there are no vibrations. This is because the sssssss sound does not need any sound from your voice box. Sounds like these are made from vibrations in your mouth.

Making Music

Musical instruments make sounds in different ways. Some instruments are tapped or banged. Others are plucked, bowed, or blown.

Vibrating Drums

If you tap a drum lightly, it vibrates slightly to produce a soft sound. But if you bang the drum hard, it produces a loud sound. A large drum vibrates slowly to produce a low note. A small drum vibrates quickly to produce a high note.

Vibrating Strings

Some instruments have strings that are plucked or bowed. This makes the strings vibrate. Stringed instruments are also **hollow.** The wood and the air inside this violin, for example, vibrate to make the sound louder.

▶ *Air is blown into wind and brass instruments. Covering the holes in this flute makes the tube of vibrating air longer or shorter. This produces different notes.*

15

Try This...

Rubber Band Guitar

Find out how stringed instruments make different notes.

You Will Need
- two or three large rubber bands • an empty tissue box
- two pencils

1 Stretch the rubber bands over the tissue box so that they lie over the hole in the top of the box.

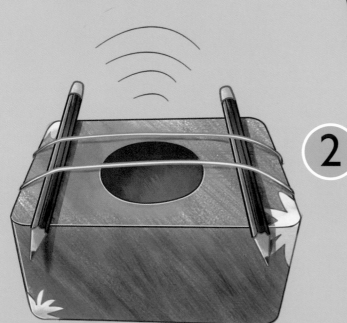

2 Push a pencil under the bands at each end of the box, to lift the bands off the box. Twang the rubber bands.

3 Try moving the pencils closer together to shorten the vibrating part of the bands. How does the sound change?

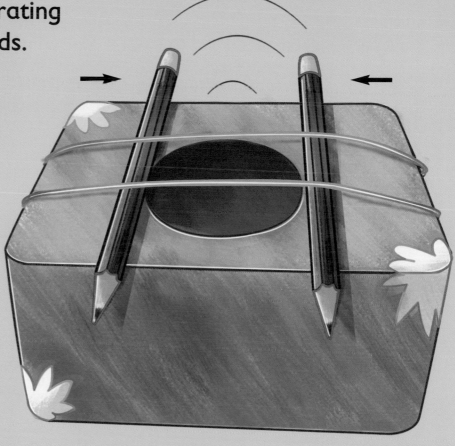

What happened?

When you twang the rubber bands, the box and the rubber bands vibrate to make a sound. The air inside the box also vibrates. This makes the sound louder. When you shorten the rubber bands, they vibrate faster and produce a higher sound.

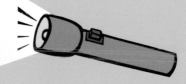

Hearing

We use our ears to hear sounds. Hearing is one of the five **senses** that help us find out about the world around us.

Our Ears

Each ear on the side of our head is the outer part of the ear. It is shaped like a cup to catch sound waves. The really important part of our ears, however, is inside our head.

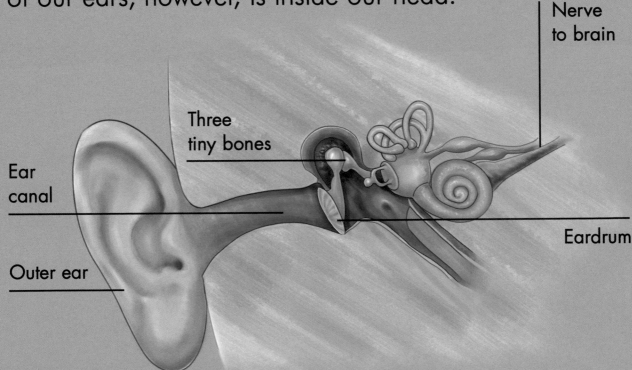

Nerve to brain

Three tiny bones

Ear canal

Outer ear

Eardrum

▲ *Sound waves travel down the ear canal and make the eardrum vibrate. This moves three tiny bones inside the ear. These vibrations send messages to the brain, which we hear as sounds.*

Taking Care of Our Ears

The **eardrum** is very thin and can be easily damaged. You should never poke objects into your ears. Very loud sounds can also damage an eardrum. This could make you **deaf.**

▶ *People who work in very noisy places wear earplugs or earmuffs to protect their ears from damage.*

Animals' Hearing

Many animals have a good sense of hearing. Animals sometimes make sounds that humans cannot hear. They can use these sounds to "talk" to each other.

Catching Sound

Some animals need a good sense of hearing to warn them of danger. Rabbits have large ears to catch as many sound waves as possible. They can also move their ears forward or backward to find out where the sound is coming from.

◀ *This rabbit has large ears to help it listen for danger.*

High and Low

If a baby mouse falls out of its nest, it makes a very high-pitched sound to attract its mother's attention. This sound is too high for us to hear. Other animals, such as whales, make very low-pitched sounds that we cannot hear.

▲ *Scientists think that elephants use their feet to feel the vibrations of very low sounds, as well as hearing them with their ears.*

Try This...

String Telephone

This will show you how sound can be guided in one direction.

You Will Need
- a pair of scissors • two yogurt cups
- a 16-foot (5-meter) length of string • two matchsticks

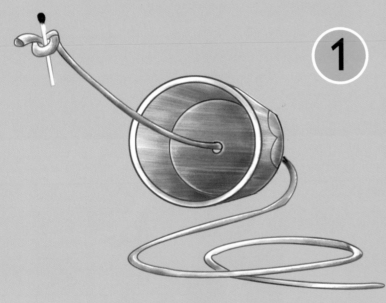

1 Ask an adult to use the scissors to make a small hole in the bottom of each yogurt cup. Thread the string through one cup. Tie a matchstick to the end of the string, so the string doesn't come out of the cup.

2 Thread the other end of the string through the other cup and tie it with a knot and matchstick as in step 1.

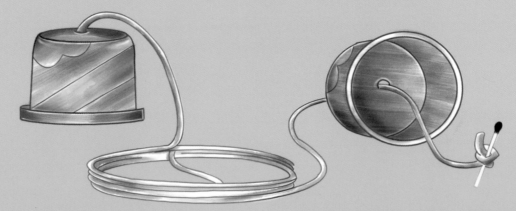

3 Hold one cup to your ear, while a friend speaks into the other cup. Make sure the string is tight. What can you hear?

What happened?

Your friend's voice will sound loud and clear in the yogurt cup. This is because the voice vibrations travel from your friend's voice along the string to the cup you are listening to. The noise will sound louder than if the vibrations just traveled through the air.

Echoes

When sound waves reach an object, some of the waves bounce back. We sometimes hear these sound waves as an **echo**.

Hearing Echoes

Smooth, hard surfaces cause sound waves to **reflect** in one direction. But we rarely hear the echo because the sound waves move so quickly. Sounds bounce off rough surfaces in different directions. This makes the echoes much quieter.

◀ Sound waves are reflected from the smooth walls of this cave. In this large space, the sound waves take a few seconds to reach our ears, so we hear the echoes very clearly.

Thunderstorms

When **lightning** flashes, it makes the air around it vibrate. This is what causes the sound of **thunder.** Echoes can change the way that thunder sounds to our ears.

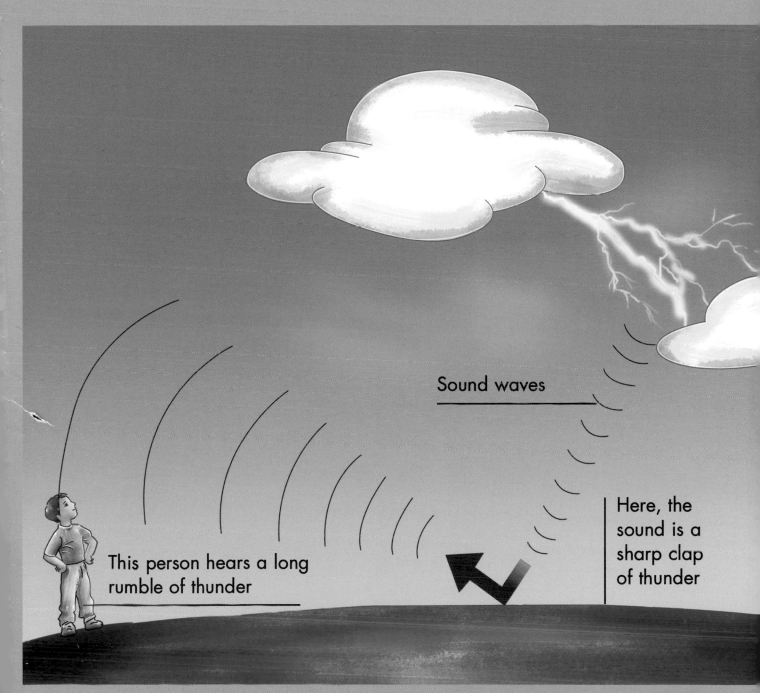

Sound waves

This person hears a long rumble of thunder

Here, the sound is a sharp clap of thunder

▲ *If you are near a storm, you will hear the thunder as a loud bang, but if you are farther away, you will hear a long rumble of thunder. This is because the sound waves reflect off the ground as echoes.*

Ultrasound

Some high-pitched sounds are too high for us to hear. We call them **ultrasounds**. These sound waves can be very useful to us.

Attracting Attention

The sound of a dog whistle is so high that humans find it difficult to hear.

▶ *A dog whistle can be used to attract a dog's attention without affecting people nearby.*

Cleaning with Sound

Ultrasound can be used to clean objects. The sound waves make a liquid vibrate so much that the dirt is removed very easily.

◀ *These old coins were found in the ground. The coins are shiny because they have been cleaned using ultrasound, which does not damage them.*

▼ *Pregnant women are often given an ultrasound scan. Ultrasound waves travel through the mother's body to give an image of how the baby is growing inside her.*

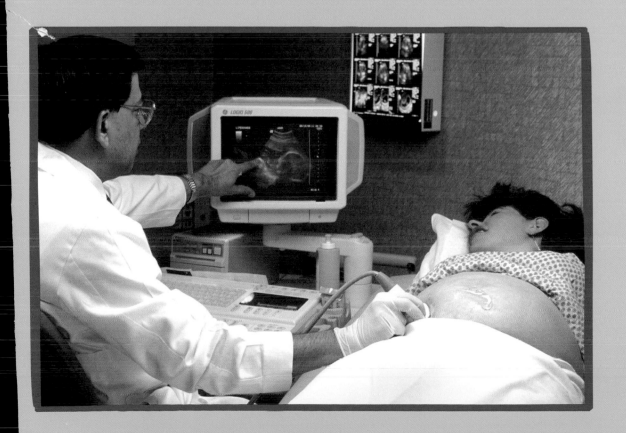

Seeing with Sound

We use our eyes to see the world around us. But did you know that humans and animals use sound to find objects, too?

Bouncing Sounds

Scientists can find out the depth of water underneath a boat. They measure how long sound waves take to travel through the water and reflect back again as echoes.

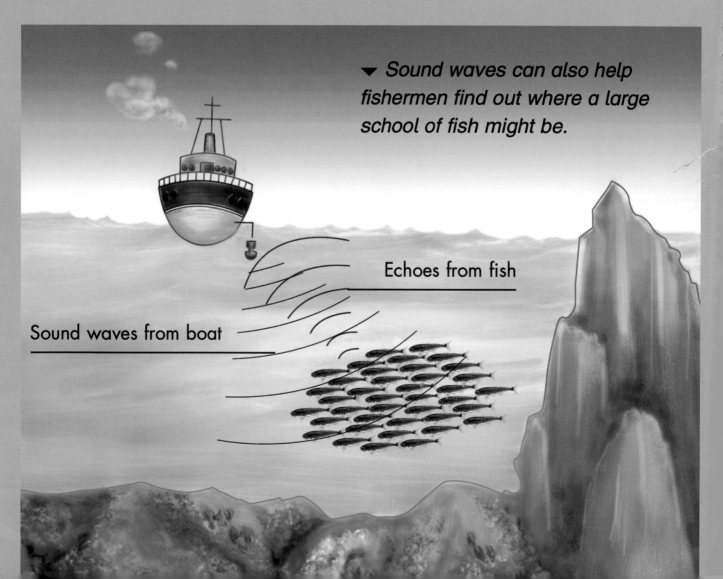

▶ *Sound waves can also help fishermen find out where a large school of fish might be.*

Echoes from fish

Sound waves from boat

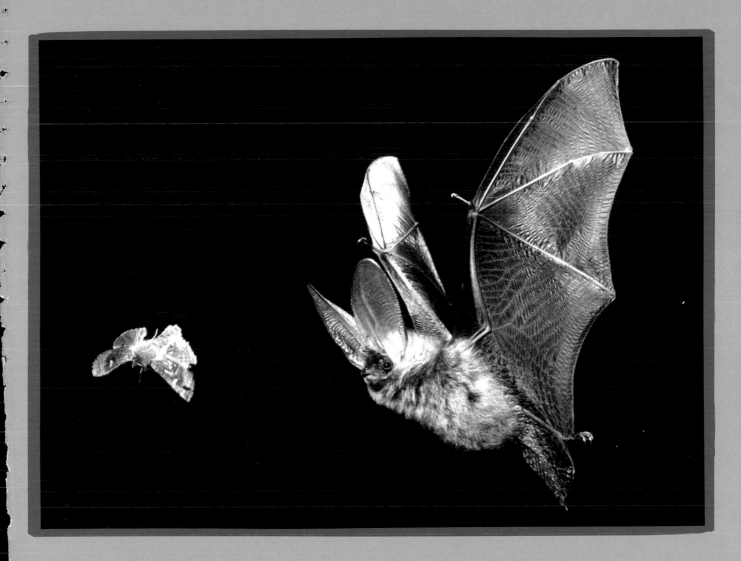

▲ *Bats make high-pitched noises when they fly at night. A bat listens to the echoes of these sound waves bouncing off different objects to find its way in the dark and to find insects to eat.*

Dolphin Clicks

Dolphins can find their way through dark, muddy water. They make clicking sounds as they swim along. These sound waves bounce off solid objects, such as the fish the dolphins like to eat. The dolphin recognizes these sounds as echoes.

Words to Remember

Communicate

To share information with other people.

Deaf

A deaf person is someone who cannot hear any sound.

Ears

The parts of our body we use to hear sound.

Eardrum

A thin piece of skin inside the ear that vibrates like a drum.

Echo

A sound that reflects off an object before it gets to our ears.

Hollow

To have a space inside. Many musical instruments are hollow.

Lightning

A flash of light caused when an electric spark jumps between clouds or from a cloud to the ground.

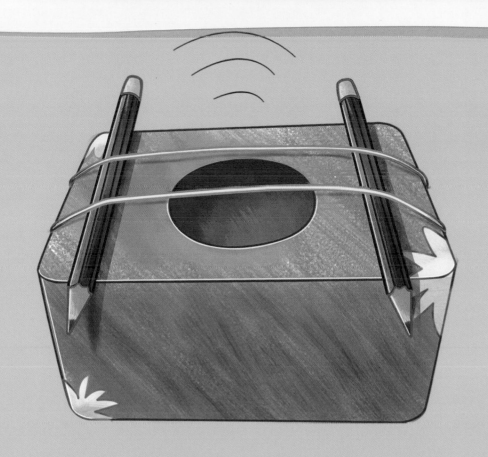

Pitch
A measure of
how high or
low different
sounds are.

Reflect
To bounce
off something.
Sound waves
bounce off
surfaces when
they reach them.

Senses
Hearing, sight,
smell, touch,
and taste are
the five senses.

Thunder
The noise made
by lightning.

Ultrasounds
Very high-
pitched sounds.

Vibrates
Moves quickly
(from side to
side or up
and down).

Voice box
An organ in the
throat that
vibrates and
produces sound
waves when air
passes through it.

Index

air 4, 6, 7, 8, 9, 10, 11, 15, 17, 23, 25

animals 5, 20, 21, 28

communication 4, 10

deafness 19

drum 14, 18

ear canal 18

eardrum 18, 19

ears 4, 7, 18, 19, 20, 21, 23, 24, 25

echo 24

musical instruments 5, 14

brass instruments 15

stringed instruments 15, 16

wind instruments 15

pitch 5, 21, 26, 29

reflect 24, 25, 28

senses 18

sound waves 4, 6, 9, 18, 20, 24, 25, 26, 27, 28, 29

speed of sound 7

thunder 25

ultrasounds 26, 27

vibrations 4, 8, 9, 13, 14, 15, 17, 18, 21, 23, 25, 27

voice 10, 11, 12, 13, 23

voice box 11, 12, 13

Web Finder

For Kids:

http://www.sci.mus.mn.us/sound/nocss/top.html

http://www.kidshealth.org/kid/body/ear_SW.html

http://www.sciencenewsforkids.org

For Teachers:

http://www.galaxy.net/~k12/sound/

http://www.cln.org/themes/sound.html

http://www.dosits.org/index.htm